Advance P

Humans Working is an unusually inspiring book on work, leadership, and innovation. Naphtali Visser, software engineer and entrepreneur, takes us into a journey of personal experiences, where he inspects work relationships from an internal point of view, as an extension of human behavior. According to Naphtali, good faith and trust point the shortest path to success. He keeps a conspicuous distance from moral principles and systems of well-being to set the foundation of his approach on the ways our mind processes information to build reality. Along these lines, working relationships based on simplicity and independent thought have far more constructive effects than rigid rules, manuals of conduct, rigorous pre-planning, and corporate obedience. Squeezing people into stereotypical roles kills imagination and the potential for creativity goes with it.

Sotirios D. Kotsopoulos, Ph.D.
Research Associate, MIT Design Lab

Humans Working is not your typical business book. This book goes much deeper than sharing organizational-level practices and strategies; it points to an understanding of human nature that applies to all people in all settings. If you are ready for deep, sustainable change that is based on mutual respect and understanding, I urge you to read *Humans Working* today.

Amy Johnson, Ph.D.
Author of *Being Human* and *The Little Book of Big Change: The No-Willpower Approach to Breaking Any Habit*

As the CEO of a fast growing company who has always tried to control a tightly-held vision, *Humans Working* has helped me shift my mindset and see that the greatest CEOs and business leaders succeed by letting go and allowing success to come through them. By humanizing your culture and team, you can cultivate an energy that is far more powerful than you can create alone. Naphtali's anecdotes hit home and relate to many circumstances and events I've experienced. I have read several books to continue to grow, but *Humans Working* has offered something different – that if I trust in the unknown; allow for something unexpected to show up; and allow the company to take on its own shape, the result can be far more powerful than I expected.

Stephan Chenette
CEO, AttackIQ

Throughout my career as a computer scientist and serial entrepreneur, I have constantly pushed for businesses to realize that the single most important thing they can do to supercharge their business is to start paying attention to the *people* they work. Simply put, engaged employees do better work and faster. People matter more than strategy and tactics. I you don't solve the human equation first, it's very difficult to get much else accomplished.

In this book, Naphtali, whom I've known for years, shows his caring nature and demonstrates his deep understanding of the truth that without a positive and happy culture, no business has a chance to be successful. If you embrace the ideas in this book, everything about your business will change.

Marty Sirkin
Co-Founder and CTO of Spoiler Alert

Humans Working goes back to the basics. Whether you're an executive of a large company or leader at a small startup, this book provides a useful mental tool to engage with the diverse interpersonal interactions that make up your day. These moments can either help push the company toward a common goal or compromise its solidarity, making each team member feel disconnected and uncommitted. Naphtali provides a compelling personal narrative, interwoven with corporate case studies, that allows you to see how seemingly complex situations, both professional and personal, can be resolved through a simple but powerful reframing of the mind – and a bit of empathy.

Saba Ghole
Co-Founder and Chief Creative Officer of NuVu Studio

Naphtali's perspective on life and business is refreshing and a reminder to keep things simple. *Humans Working* is a necessary read and it reiterates the importance of something you typically pay little attention to; your mind. You'll be happy you read this.

Louie Balasny
Co-Founder and Managing Director of botkeeper

Humans Working has let me re-appraise what's important in the day-to-day of running a creative agency – the challenges of high pressure deadlines, demanding clients, changing objectives, and the need to always be "creatively on" – all of which can be handled with far more grace and assuredness by taking note, and being inspired by Naphtali's book.

Thomas O'Connell
Founder and Chief Creative Officer, Heart

Humans Working is a game-changer! Unlike most business books, you will not find strategies, tools, or techniques you need to follow. Instead, Naphtali points us to the most important thing for any business to thrive: what's already inside us. With wit, humor, and personal stories, Naphtali takes you on a personal journey to ignite the spark inside your business and even your personal life. Read this book the first time for information and read it again for a transformation!

Amir Karkouti
CEO of Surf Brothers Teriyaki

Most business books share tactics that have worked for them. This book points to principles that work for everyone.

David Westerman
Men's Coach

For over twenty years, I have known Naphtali as a vendor, consultant, business partner, and friend. Naphtali's personal journey and growth continue to fuel ideas and opportunities that he has effectively shared in this book. His ability to clearly communicate his own experience and distill this thinking and transformative mindset has allowed me, and many others that I know, to access and achieve their untapped potential.

The message in this book is, at its core, pointing to what you already know, yet is quite contrary to much of the typical advice of the business world. Tapping one's own, or someone else's, potential does not come from incentives or consequences, but rather from engaging with the fundamental experience that it is to be human: shared, collaborative, honest, and fair.

Naphtali's take on business, management, and being a whole person gets at the core of what it means to be a "human working". I encourage everyone to read this book and to look inward, act outward, and receive the benefits of these shifts in mindset and behavior to be a fundamentally happier and better person, employee, and business leader.

Timothy Driscoll
Senior Director, Innovation & Digital Health Accelerator at Boston Children's Hospital

Simplicity is beauty. Sometimes you come across something that is so trivial you just want to smack yourself for not getting it yourself. This book shows where problems that you (and just about every company) have been dealing with your whole life come from; how you've been compounding them; and presents a solution that seems to work every single time.

Hermann Kelley
Senior Principal Lead at Symantec

Naphtali is committed to the essence of human nature and to kindness. He prescribes no tools or tips or checklists to follow. He leads you to achieve clarity of yourself and your situation. We all make assumptions that we believe are obvious and true. But, without realizing it, we can let those assumptions impose false barriers to achieving what we want to achieve. Naphtali has a deep understanding of how business works – and the tech industry specifically – which adds to the calm confidence you develop as you read Humans Working. In this book, plenty of practical specifics evolve out of his pointing to you toward clarity through a simple understanding of how the mind works.

Jesse Nahan
Technology Executive and Entrepreneur

HUMANS WORKING

Why culture and mindset
beat strategy

Naphtali Visser

Nafico, Inc. – Brookline, MA

Copyright © 2018 Naphtali Visser

All rights reserved.

This book or any portion thereof may not be copied, reproduced, transmitted in any form, or used in any manner whatsoever without the express written permission of the author.

Disclaimer: This book provides a point-of-view on the way that the human mind works. Whatever you choose to take from this book or implement in your business or personal life is up to you. Nothing in this book should be construed as business or legal advice. I'm a writer; not a lawyer, therapist or other licensed professional. Follow your heart with a good dose of your trusted professionals' advice.

Printed in the United States of America
First Printing, 2018

ISBN [Paperback]: 978-0-9998506-0-2
ISBN [Kindle]: 978-0-9998506-1-9

Nafico, Inc.
1732 1st Ave., Suite 26199
New York, NY 10128

Author: naphtalivisser.com
Corporate Consulting: humansworking.co
Book Companion: humansworkingbook.com

Cover art and author photograph by Amro Arida.

Table of Contents

Introduction	i
Chapter One: Why Culture Matters	**1**
How I Got Here	2
About This Book	7
The Short Version	11
What It's Not	14
Why Culture Matters	16
Chapter Two: The Inside-Out Understanding	**21**
Our Experience is Created from the Inside-Out, Moment-to-Moment	23
Separate Realities	26
Resilience	33
Guidance	40
Chapter Three: Business Implications	**49**
The Source of All (Business) Problems and Solutions	51
Rapport	56
Management	62
Dealing with Bad Behavior	65
Deadlines, Quotas and Stress	71
Productivity	78
Recruiting and Hiring	81
Interviewing	88
Innovation	92
Chapter Four: Parting Thoughts	**100**
Epilogue	101
Epilogue #2: I Have a Dream	104
Next Steps	107
Sources	108
Acknowledgements	110

Introduction

What if everything you thought you knew about developing a strong culture came from an innocent misunderstanding of how the mind works? What if everything that you've been continually told about all the work you have to "do" to be successful, create a strong culture and a successful company was incorrect? What if there was a much simpler way? What if so-called "culture best practices" were precisely *the cause* of the demise of so many companies? What if most companies' approach to developing a strong culture is actually antithetical to having one?

What if a simple, straightforward understanding of how the mind works was all you really needed to build a culture that inspired innovation, productivity, fierce loyalty and the ability to continually solve complex business problems without having to hire expensive consultants or get more training? What if you never needed to read another book, take another online course of "proven strategies" (about culture or anything else), or buy into someone else's success story, and certainly never needed to attend another seminar to jump up and down like a kangaroo on peyote?

What if I could help you see clearly for yourself that your mind is naturally wired for success and that it's possible to develop a world-class culture using only the tools that are already available to you, and in fact, have always been available? How would you feel if you really knew, in the same way that you know that the sun comes up every day, that you already have everything you need to inspire such a culture, grow a business, and have a huge impact on the world at the same time?

Come on in; let's join each other on a magical journey.

Chapter One

Why Culture Matters

How I Got Here

In 1997, when I was 23, I started an Internet software consulting company. To be frank, I started it mostly out of frustration of the way that other companies I'd worked for (mostly prominent "interactive agencies") treated people. While I knew that it'd be fun to create software in the early days of the Internet, my primary goal was to create a fun atmosphere – a clubhouse, if you will – that people would love coming to every day. I assumed that if that were the case, we'd be able to find interesting clients and do some interesting work and make a good living at it. What started as a one-man company organically grew to a six person organization operating out of the living room of my one-bedroom apartment, to a group of 15 amazing folks in a "proper" loft-style office in downtown Boston.

We ran a successful business for four years. We were profitable, provided very competitive salaries, great benefits, and a really fun atmosphere. We worked on projects that, for the most part, we all found interesting and challenging. In my opinion, we fared better than a similar company across the street from ours, that raised over $100MM in venture capital, had some massive clients, and still managed to go out of business before they could turn a profit.

After four wonderful years, our biggest client went out of business because their promised second round of funding didn't materialize. Consequently, they weren't able to pay us a huge amount of money they owed us, for work we'd already completed. I was shocked and clearly disappointed, but in my typically idealistic way, I knew that within a year or so we could recover. But, a week later, all of our other, smaller yet consistent and substantive clients, called and told us that "because of the economy" (it was just before 9/11/2001, and the economy was in a tailspin) they were "re-evaluating," and as a result, had no more projects for us.

It was at that point that I knew that our business was no longer viable. With no money in the company bank account, less than $500 to my name, and payroll of $40,000 due in 2 days, it was clearly time to shut the doors. I summoned the team – 10 people at the time – to our conference room, and with tears, told them that I loved them, that we'd had a great run, but it was time to go home. There was no other option. I told them that the paycheck I owed them wouldn't be forthcoming and that their health insurance and other benefits were canceled, effective immediately. I told them that I'd do whatever I could to help them find another job (which was tough at the time), that I hoped we could all stay tight as friends, but there was just no more viability for our company.

It took an interminable 60 seconds or so for anyone to say anything. Eventually, Jim, who had a bit of a reputation as a wise-ass, said, "I'll stay." I wasn't sure if he was being sincere or sarcastic, so while I acknowledged his kindness, I completely dismissed the content.

A few seconds later, Mark piped up with, "Me too. I'll stay." Then Thomas, in his confident, deep voice: "Me too. You'll come up with something, you always do."

One at a time, around the smallish dark wood conference table (which I now use as my desk), each of them said they'd stay. I had no idea where this amazingly generous gesture came from, nor what they really meant by it, but I had (and still have) no words to express my feeling at that moment.

I told them that I had no idea what they meant and that I was convinced they were just caught up in the adrenaline of the moment, but that I was willing to "run with it" and see what happened. I suspected that by the next morning they'd all have changed their minds. But, sure enough, the next day, and every day for two months, they all came to work, on time, and did whatever I asked them to do. To be honest, I'm not really sure what they worked on. We had a light trickle of client work but not enough to keep any one of them, no less all of them, busy.

They stayed for two months, without pay, until we landed a new client – the largest one, by far, that we'd ever gotten! Soon after that win, and only because of it, we were able to sell the company. In the sale of the company, I negotiated only two points: a) the entire staff (as opposed to a handful of employees they had wanted to cherry-pick) would be hired by the new company; and b) everyone would get a raise. This was definitely pushing my luck, since so many people, even programmers, were being laid off every day; but to have done anything less would have been traitorous. We merged with the other company, and while that experience came with its own set of challenges, it was so amazing to feel that together we'd made something that looked a lot like lemonade.

Since then, I've known that I could help companies create strong cultures that would foster loyalty and create more prosperity for everyone involved. As I've progressed along this journey, I've noticed that by helping companies develop strong cultures, I could also help many thousands of people enjoy – even love – their work.

As I've continued on this journey, I've seen that teaching the "inside-out understanding," which I use as the basis for my work, can have ripple effects for the families and communities of the folks who work at these companies (and hopefully much further).

About This Book

This book was inspired by my experiences as the owner of a few businesses and as a "individual contributor" or "senior manager" at several other organizations. It's definitely not about the things that I've done to garner success, nor does it point toward duplicating the environments of other seemingly wildly successful companies. It's most certainly not a step-by-step process, a set of "hacks", or a "recipe book" of things to "do" to create a picture-perfect culture.

Instead, I am going to continually point you "inside" to the brilliance already inside you. I promise you that whatever prescription you need is already inside you. I'll offer an understanding of the *only source* of a great culture and I'll illustrate this understanding by sharing many real-world examples of operating a business, mostly from companies that I've started, worked for, or consulted with.

Even though this isn't a book of tactics, some tactics definitely have their place in business – I'm not saying they don't. But, when you have clarity – when your mind is clear, and you have an understanding of where your experience of life is coming from – the tactics usually take care of themselves. Clarity brings you a set of tactics that were not previously available and a way to execute them with drastically less stress than trying to execute someone else's plan. Sometimes, our reliance on others' "prescriptions" points us away from where creativity, brilliance, confidence and inspiration really come from. *They're all an inside job!*

The "understanding" I'm speaking of is an understanding of how the human mind (our "operating system", if you like) works and how *it creates our experience of life*. My hope is that at some point while reading this book, you'll have an insight – one of those "a-ha" moments where you see something new – not intellectually, but rather in your soul (or perhaps your belly).

I know that what I share is contrary to popular opinion, and to almost all other business advice. In some cases, it might seem at first like complete nonsense. If you focus on the words, you will likely find an argument, and it may be hard to see what I'm pointing to. But, if you can slow down a bit, look beyond the words, and try to "feel" what I'm sharing, rather than be quick to judge whether or not you agree with my "approach," something new might show up for you, and that could change *everything*! I promise, the magic isn't in these pages – it's in you.

I'm hoping that as a business leader, you'll be open to seeing something new, just as you likely do every day in many other aspects of your job. I'm sure you regularly try to come up with new, perhaps disruptive ways of doing something or inventing something that no one has yet dreamed of. The same place that those big ideas come from is where insights for cultivating a strong culture and solving very difficult business problems will come from.

I promise you that you can affect a dramatic shift in your company's culture, and in turn, the success of your business, simply through a new understanding of what's actually driving your own experience and the experiences of everyone around you. It's actually much simpler than you might think.

With this deeper understanding of the human operating system (and some real-world business examples to illustrate it), you may choose to implement some new policies, or you may notice, as so many have, that things just start to change on their own, seemingly magically. One thing I'm sure of is this: whatever needs "doing" will become readily apparent and doing it will seem very natural.

Though this book is ostensibly about improving corporate culture, grasping the understanding that I'm describing here will serve you in business far beyond evolving a culture. Seemingly intractable business problems may all of a sudden look simple. Beyond that, the implications for affecting personal friendships, romantic relationships, interactions with your children, and just about every other life situation, are real and endless.

A Note on Language

Throughout this book, I often use the pronoun "we" to refer to your company, my company, or anyone else's company. I do this, in part, because I want to go on this journey with you, but also because we're all in this together. Really.

A Note on Stories

In the outlined boxes throughout the book, I include stories that attempt to most vividly illustrate the concept of each section. In some cases, I chose stories that came from places other than "business," both because they were better stories and to illustrate how the understanding I point to in this book shows up everywhere! And, of course, the names have been changed.

The Short Version

Everything that I'm pointing to in this book can be summarized as follows:

- Thought *creates* our experience, moment-to-moment, "from the inside-out." Our experience is created through us, not *to* or *at* us.
- We are all naturally wired for success.

You know that saying, "It is what it is?" Well, "it" doesn't exist on its own. Your experience of "it" is created, moment-to-moment, through the power of thought. Some people call this "perception", but it's more than that.

Consider that guy at work who is just a complete jerk – the one who's so frustrating to be around because of his arrogance and stupidity. You know the one I mean, right? As it turns out, your experience of him *is created by your mind, and does not come from him at all!* That's why, on some days, you'll want to wring his neck; sometimes, you'll think he's actually not a bad guy; other days you'll think that he's kind of dumb but doing the best he can; and still others you won't even think of him and consequently, will have absolutely no experience of him.

If you truly see that as true, 100% of the time, then feel free to skip the rest of this book. If not, my hope is that by the time you finish this book, or after navigating life with this new understanding, that you will clearly see this truth. Though, as clearly as you see this truth, sometimes, it's still going to look like life is happening to you. And that's fine. Just know that it's not.

Here are some potential implications of this understanding:

- You never need to be afraid of your experience. You can stop worrying and chasing all of your "What if..." scenarios down a rabbit hole.

- You don't have to be alarmed when you have crappy feelings. You only need to understand where they're coming from and that your mind will "heal" on its own, without intervention.

- You don't need to fix anything, since there's nothing to fix. You're always right where you're supposed to be, and you're always "doing" life "right."

- You don't need to intervene to settle or heal your mind, just as a pond requires no intervention to settle itself after being disrupted by a pebble or boulder.

- You don't have to "manage change" or expend energy trying to "engage" employees.
- You don't have to "manage" people or problems; rather, just understand where all business problems come from.
- You don't need more time management strategies or a better calendar or a more efficient assistant.

What It's Not

While some of what I describe in this book may seem like something you've heard before, please know that I'm not suggesting "positive thinking" or "mindfulness." Your mind has a very strong built-in "immune system" to heal itself when you're feeling insecure, depressed, or having any other feelings you don't like. You don't need to manage this system through positive thinking, mindfulness, or anything else.

It's also not a religious spiritual paradigm or practice. Pieces may seem like they come from Buddhism or Taoism (or even Judaism, Christianity or Islam). While I agree that most major religions, at their core, point to the same place that I am, what I'm describing here has no dogma attached to it. There are absolutely no rules and there's certainly no right or wrong way to do life. As Michael Neill, the author whose book first pointed me to this understanding, wrote, "You couldn't do life wrong if you tried." All I'm describing is how the human operating system works and how you can use that understanding to benefit you in business and elsewhere.

It's not about "magical thinking" – that is, believing that happy thoughts will bring riches to your doorstep. There is no "secret" here. It's also not about managing your karma.

While my *personal* hope is that humans will use their resources, this understanding included, for the betterment of mankind, my personal preference really has nothing to do with the understanding itself. The implications of this understanding are different for each person.

Why Culture Matters

Culture is not something that is separate from or adjacent to your company. Culture is like a living organism – constantly growing and evolving, whether or not you're paying attention to it. It feeds off of any energy it finds, whether "positive" or "negative" and has no preference as to how it evolves. Culture is not something that you think about once you've developed your product and have some paying customers. Culture is not what happens when all your ducks are finally in a row.

In this book, I'm not prescribing a certain type of culture. I don't care about a "customer first" culture; a culture of trust, love, or transparency; or even an "every man for himself" culture.

What I am suggesting is that the "strength" of any culture is directly correlated to the extent that our team "gets" (in the same way that you "get" a joke) that reality is created moment-to-moment through thought.

A strong culture naturally breeds loyalty and the ability to consistently weather "storms" you're bound to encounter. (In this book you'll learn that storms aren't actually real – they only exist as a reflection of your state of mind.) When problems do arise, they often seem to sort themselves out, and even when it looks like there's something we need to do to fix them, whatever needs to be done seems to present itself in the moment.

A strong culture is also marked by our team's ability to continually innovate – though after a while, it will seem that "innovation" shows up all time. Continual innovation is needed not only when creating new products but also when selling to "difficult" customers; dealing with product failures, recalls and economic downturns; and well, pretty much all the time. Business is a game of continual iteration and innovation and understanding that innovation comes from inside, not anywhere else, is what can catapult one company past another.

Imagine that your staff's ability to be "productive" wasn't variable based on the circumstances of the moment. Imagine if annoying clients, intense deadlines or quotas, good or bad market conditions or "personality quirks" couldn't affect that ability. Imagine if your employees' sense of fear, obligation, or desire to "prove" could disappear. Imagine what would happen if your staff's mindset shifted from *having* to stay at work to *wanting* to stay at work, without you having to offer incentives or threaten punishments. Imagine what might happen when your employees' daydreams about work shift from that giant pile of work they *have to do* to generating creative, innovative ideas and the work they *get to do*. And what if that was possible without *you* having to *do* anything?

It seems that companies that possess this understanding, regardless of their product or service, not only have greater "business" (i.e. financial) success, but also have a greater impact on the world.

Here are some concrete benefits of a strong culture:

- You can solve problems you've been struggling with for a long time, even if you've already tried expensive consultants.
- You can notice that there's opportunity in a downturn, even if you don't immediately know what that specific opportunity is.
- People become more loving, tolerant, peaceful, engaged, and productive.
- Problems seem to disappear by themselves.
- Loyalty, personal growth, and company growth happen without having to focus on them.
- "Bad morale" never seems like something that needs to be fixed.

- A sense of ease, clarity and flow; not of having to grit your teeth to get through.

Nordstrom

Nordstrom is very successful by just about any business measure and is known for having outstanding customer service. Many books (and Nordstrom themselves) point to their commitment to outstanding customer service. But, they haven't "built" a culture around that. They haven't developed rules, procedures, mantras, or anything else of the sort.

Nordstrom spokesperson Tara Darrow, when asked about their lack of focus on "culture" said, "We don't have a thick manual telling our employees what they can and cannot do... we just ask them to use good judgment in all situations. We hope this philosophy not only empowers employees to provide the highest level of service to our customers, but also inspires them and helps build a great workplace."

That's it. Trust that people will do the right thing. Usually they will, and sometimes they won't. Even when they mess up, trust them. That understanding is what will naturally evolve into what looks like a strong culture.

I've seen the Nordstrom "manual," and if it weren't for a dozen or so pages that outlined concrete benefits like health insurance, it'd be ridiculous to call it a manual at all. Here's all the meat:

"Our number one goal is to provide outstanding customer service. Set both your personal and professional goals high. We have great confidence in your ability to achieve them, so our employee handbook is very simple. We have only one rule: Use good judgment in all situations. Please feel free to ask your department manager, store manager, or Human Resources any questions at any time."

Chapter Two

The Inside-Out Understanding

Throughout this book, I'll continue to point to the understanding that the mind only works one way, all the time. That is, the mind creates our experience from moment-to-moment; our experience is not created by the circumstances of our world. That is, our experience is created "from the inside-out," hence the "inside-out understanding."

In this section, we'll dig a bit deeper into this understanding, and in the following section, we'll discuss the business (and some personal) implications that a deep knowing of this understanding can provide.

There is considerable overlap among the tenets I describe in this section. Guidance, resilience and clarity aren't really separate concepts – I'm just pointing to the same idea from various angles so that you have a greater chance of seeing something new.

Our Experience is Created from the Inside-Out, Moment-to-Moment

It often looks like whatever we are feeling in the moment is attributable to something that's happening in the world around us.

It may seem like we get really annoyed when that guy from accounting comes and asks us for our timesheet four times in a row on a Friday afternoon when we're just trying to wrap up and head out for the weekend. It sometimes looks like we become anxious when our boss yells at us. When we win a contract or get a raise, it might look like those events bring us joy.

But, it's not those circumstances that are creating those feelings, at all, ever. Our experience of *every* situation comes to us through the power of thought. In each moment, thought is creating a vivid picture for us, which we look at and believe to be true. Thought often comes so quickly that we don't even notice it. Thought is responsible for *continually creating an experience of the world that we live in*.

Because thought is always changing and often shows up without us even noticing, our experience of any situation will also be variable, based on our thinking in that moment. When we're feeling connection and a sense of being "in love" with the world around us, we're likely to have a much different experience of anything that happens than when it looks like the world is a horrible place.

So what *is* this thought that I speak of? It's not the handful of conscious thoughts that are in your head at the moment; rather it's the "power of thought." As of yet, no one is really sure where thought is created, yet it's clear that *we (or at least our conscious minds) aren't creating it*. In the same way that we aren't in control of making our heart beat or forcing a cut to heal, we really aren't in control of this *thought energy* that's always flowing through us.

Imagine a time, perhaps when you were in the shower or out for a walk in the woods, that a brilliant idea just popped into your head. Maybe it was the answer to a crossword you couldn't figure out; or an idea on how to make Thanksgiving much more pleasant this year; or finding a new cure for cancer. Did you have to do anything for that to happen? Of course not, it just showed up, in the same way that your body's ability to heal a cut just shows up when it needs to.

As an analogy, think of thought like a weather system that's constantly passing through us. Sometimes there are lots of dark clouds; sometimes, nothing but sun. And occasionally, even on a sunny day, there's a quick thunderstorm. While we may have preferences for one sort of weather or another, we realize that there's really nothing that any of us can do to "fix" the weather. Yucky weather is as normal a part of the system as beautiful weather is, and if we don't like it, all we need to do is wait for the storm to pass.

When we're feeling crappy, it's simply because of crappy thought passing through us, just as a storm passes through the sky. There's no way to "change" your thoughts or to "focus on the good ones" – we just don't have that power. We're wired to have ups and downs.

Spending time chasing an "up" feeling when we're feeling down is trying to fix something that's not broken in the first place. The "down" state is just as normal as the "up" state.

Yet, it seems to me, the less we "hang on" to negative feelings when they arise, the more we seem to drift back to shore, to an "up" state.

Separate Realities

Because we experience our thinking rather than experiencing the events or circumstances that are happening around us, each of us has a different experience of the world – and in fact, each of us has a unique experience of every situation.

We see this, for example, when we go to the movies with a friend. We might love the movie, while our friend hates it. The same circumstance renders a different experience due to the variable nature of thought.

In business, after winning a big contract, some of us might have thoughts of additional revenue and experience joy. Some might have thoughts of all of the late nights that will be required, and experience stress. Some may have absolutely no thinking around it, and therefore will have no experience of the win.

Or let's say that your boss yells at you and a colleague. You may perceive that yelling as demeaning and threatening while your colleague may perceive it as a challenge to excel. You may not even perceive it as yelling, but rather just a loud pep talk!

Here's an example that's a bit more complex. Let's say that you're the CEO of a company that holds a staff meeting every Monday at 8:00 AM sharp. Joe is often late and usually has some lame excuse like "traffic". On one particular Monday, Joe shows up 40 minutes late and you notice as he walks into the room that you feel redness in your face and tightness in your chest. As you stand up to give him a verbal lashing, *without you doing anything*, something in you shifts and as you notice something very subtle in his expression, you ask if everything is okay. He says that he was in a car accident and though his car was totaled, he called a cab to get to work as soon as possible. Your anger switches to compassion as you offer him any assistance he needs.

The circumstance didn't change (he was still very late), yet your experience shifted significantly. Even before he'd mentioned the car accident, your thought may have shifted based on something you sensed.

But, several people are whispering amongst themselves that Joe isn't trustworthy and probably made up the whole story about the car accident. Their thought created a completely different experience than yours.

Others believe Joe's story, but think he probably deserved it since he's often angry at work and it was likely his road rage that caused the accident. Their thinking created yet another experience.

And some people who were just staring at their phones when Joe walked in perhaps had no experience of Joe's lateness or his accident.

Each person in the room had a unique experience when Joe walked into the room, based on their thinking in the moment, and potentially several unique experiences as their thinking shifted. It's important to note that their thinking "came" to them – they didn't "make" it.

Isn't it strange that in a big room of several people, presented with the exact same set of "facts," each person had his or her own experience? And each person's experience – their "version" of the story – seemed 100% true to them!

So, what's important to notice here? We could try to dissect each person's thoughts and analyze *what they were thinking* to try to tie those thoughts to their experience. But it's much more powerful just to recognize that **experience is being created due to the fact that we're thinking.** Even if it were possible to control our thinking, we don't need to. Thoughts come and go, and when they do, our experiences change.

"Inventing" Google

We used to think the earth was flat, that the sun revolved around the earth, that the universe wasn't expanding, that germs had nothing to do with disease, and that we couldn't generate new brain cells. And we really believed those things to be absolutely true.

Throughout history, we have consistently been wrong about what we perceive. Today, with such honed analytical skills and a virtually unlimited source of information at our fingertips, it seems as if we could no longer make a foolish mistake like thinking that the world is flat. Yet, we do, all the time.

In 1996, the company I was working at hired a 23 year old (the same age as me and many of the other developers) to co-manage the technology department. We all mocked him for his lack of years and experience, but mostly we mocked him for his laughably ridiculous idea: to collect all of the information in the world, put it in a database, and build a natural language search engine so that you could ask it questions like, "Who was the 35th president?" or more likely, "Who serves the best burger in Boston?" We came up with every reason why this would never be possible. How would you even find all that information? What about all the information that was hidden away in books in back rooms of libraries? How could you possibly determine what was worthwhile information versus junk, and how could you really understand what a user "meant" by their search?

As early as 2007, Google's features fully represented what he'd imagined; and now, in 2017, Google seems to know what you want before you ask. What seemed absolutely impossible to many (even us techies) seemed like just a hop, skip and a jump away to someone else.

This is obviously important to remember from an innovation standpoint. But more importantly, it clearly illustrates how real each person's reality seems to them, even when it seems completely *unreal* to us.

Root Cause Analysis (Who's To Blame?)

After every large project at any company I've worked at, we (the techies) would inevitably talk about all of the things that everyone else did wrong. Sales had promised too much without asking us first; marketing didn't even understand what the project entailed anyway; and of course, the graphics folks didn't meet their deadlines, so we had to scramble.

I'm sure that in every other corner of the office, each of those departments was having their own version of the same meeting, listing all of the reasons why our department didn't create exactly what they'd asked for, and lamenting that we'd be the reason for the company's decline.

And the thing is, we were all right, in a way. We all *created* a reality, based on our own thinking in the moment that seemed incredibly real to us. So real, that any other reality created through others' thinking seemed incredibly un-real.

Resilience

All humans are resilient – we always get back up even when it seems like we won't be able to. Built into each and every one of us, regardless of our histories, biochemical imbalances, socioeconomic status, or anything else, is an extremely powerful system that always resets the mind back to a neutral, or natural, state. Just as your hand knows how to heal when you slice into it while chopping parsley (I've done that on more than a dozen occasions), your mind knows how to heal itself when it's in a crappy state. Just as you don't need to do anything in order for your hand to heal (perhaps other than keep it free of germs and gunk), you need to do nothing for your mind to heal (other than not kicking up more thinking).

We've all experienced "bad" situations – losing a loved one, getting divorced, closing a business, or being involved in a war. And yet, each of us has been able to continue with life, without having to "do" anything in order to heal, even if healing seemed to take a long time. We may have not gotten through every situation in the exact way we would have preferred, but we got through. That's resilience. It's built in. The power of resilience will always save us, if we just give it half a chance to do its magic.

Imagine how many people operate from a place of not knowing that resilience has their back. As a result, they may think that they have to always protect themselves and their futures. How many people don't express their ideas because they think that their dumb idea might get them fired, without the benefit of knowing that resilience will have their back. How many people don't start a business or otherwise follow their dreams for fear of failing?

Think about how much freer we all could be if we didn't fear our experience! What could change if we knew that we'd be okay, no matter what; that the system of resilience would always come to our rescue, even if we couldn't see how that might happen?

Modern neurology points to the fact that athletes that perform at an incredibly high level often have the same strength and conditioning as their peers, but what makes one able to perform "off the charts" is their ability to "take the brakes off". What would change if all of us were able to take the brakes off, knowing that no matter what, we'll be fine?

For every "problem" that shows up in life there are so many potential solutions. Many of them show up precisely at the moment that we need them, without ever having planned for them, and often look like solutions we never could have possibly imagined.

Consider the story at the beginning of this book. Just when I thought that there was no other option than to shut down our business, something that I couldn't have predicted in a million years showed up. Ten guys stood up and said they'd work for free until we could get back on our feet. That is precisely how this system of resilience works! When we're willing and open to seeing it, it shows up, every time.

Love Among Guns and Mugging

A few years ago, I decided to spend a month in Detroit working on a photography project. For several years, I've been photographing cityscapes, industrial scenes and water, mostly at night. Detroit seemed to be calling my name. Through a very unexpected gesture, my friend connected me with his cousins who live just outside Detroit, whom I lived with for a month (and made some life-long friends at the same time). Through the same friend, I was also connected to a high-ranking officer in the Detroit Police

Department. After looking at my portfolio, he very generously pointed me toward places he thought I'd be interested in photographing. He suggested the old Packard plant, and assured me that during daylight hours it was very safe to be there.

On my very first day in Detroit – a bright, sunny day – I went to the Packard plant at 3PM. I set up my camera on a tripod in the middle of a large paved lot adjacent to the old plant. Within 2 minutes, after having only made 3 pictures, I noticed a guy walking toward me. He was tall, muscular, and African American, wearing a navy blue hoodie with the hood pulled over his head, obscuring some of his face. I hoped that he was just making a short cut through the lot, but as he made eye contact, I knew that he was coming for me.

The adrenaline started to flow. I'm not a big guy (quite the opposite) and certainly not a "tough" guy. Because of the geography of the space, there was nowhere to run; I knew I just had to deal with it.

As he approached, he pulled out a massive handgun and said, "Give me all your cash or you're gonna die right here!"

In that moment, something in me shifted. For some reason, whatever fear was in me disappeared, and it shifted to something that you could call love, kindness or understanding. I wasn't pleased with his behavior, but still saw the humanness in him. I saw *that*, not *how*, we are the same. I was 95% sure that I'd get through the ordeal unharmed, but I had a deep feeling that even if I were injured or killed, I'd still be okay. Strange, I know.

I didn't do anything to get to that feeling of love or feeling that I'd be okay. I didn't practice a special breathing technique, recite mantras, or pray; it just happened. Looking back, I now understand that something helped me to see him for *who he really is*, not his circumstance, race, size, or the fact that he was sporting a hefty handgun. And in that moment, everything shifted.

From there, our encounter was terse yet conversational; not confrontational. I ended up forfeiting my cash, wallet and phone, but negotiated to get my wallet back after letting him take the credit cards. Afterwards, there were some physical side effects – I was a bit shaky from the adrenaline – but that faded pretty quickly. I wrote a several-page account of what had happened, in detail, as a way to "process." But there were no lingering effects beyond that. I'm not afraid of going back to Detroit or other "bad neighborhoods." I'm not afraid of being mugged or of violence.

When I think back on this experience, I hope that that guy now has a better life than he did when we met.

How powerful could it be just to know that this level of understanding and resilience is available, all the time, without doing anything, even if we sometimes slip up and don't see it? What could change if we could see each other – our employees, bosses, vendors, customers, etc. – as human first? What could change if we knew that even if someone *really* did something crappy to us that it didn't have to affect us negatively? What if we could see that when someone is "acting out" (and it looks like they're being aggressive *toward* us), that usually it has nothing to do with us; rather, likely, they're just suffering through their own thoughts a bit?

Guidance

It seems to me that there's something that's shared among all of us, that connects us all together. It's what makes the earth spin, the sun rise, cuts heal, and feelings shift. It's what makes those thousands of thoughts appear in our heads randomly and makes brilliant thoughts show up in the shower, without us doing anything.

You can call it the "subconscious" (which may exist entirely in our brain, or perhaps even outside of us, depending on whom you ask), or "god" or whatever you like – I call it a "universal intelligence." Knowing that we can tap into that intelligence at any time we like (and knowing that it's always there, even when we forget) is extremely powerful.

Practically, this guidance can show up in many ways. For example, when we're trying to invent something new, sometimes a completely formed idea comes to us in a dream. Other times, a zygote of an idea appears, and as we work on it, fresh thoughts show up (seemingly on their own schedule) and guide us along a path toward completion.

I have seen far too many companies rush toward what they believe to be a great idea, only to miss out on so many opportunities along the way; or perhaps even worse, don't pursue an idea they're passionate about simply because they can't immediately see how it would be completed or how the market would respond to it. Personally, I can tell you of so many times that I've started a programming project that I thought was impossible only to realize halfway through that in fact what I feared would be the hardest (or most impossible) part was actually quite trivial once I *just got started.*

A Lifesaving Human Chain

I recently read a true story of two young boys who were caught in a riptide while swimming. When seven others tried to swim to save them, they too got caught in the riptide. From there, seemingly spontaneously, a group of 80 people formed a human chain and within minutes, rescued all nine of them.

Where'd this idea come from? If everyone on that beach had read every book or blog of "tips" on how to escape a riptide, I am pretty confident that none of them would have read about this solution!

And yet, it was implemented almost instantaneously, without prior planning, without a brainstorming session, without anyone declaring herself the leader, and with no understanding of any of the participants' personalities, management styles, communication styles, etc.

What might happen if we depended on this sort of guidance more often in our day-to-day corporate existence? Clearly, it works even when the stakes are really high.

Hiring Two Guys, Simultaneously

Several months after starting my consulting company, one of our clients went out of business, and there was a programmer there who had been laid off. At the time, our company was just me and a buddy. We were getting a bit busier, so I asked the guy who'd been laid off if he'd like to work with us part time. He said he could for a little while, but really needed a full-time job.

Somehow, over the course of a few days, I convinced myself that somehow it'd be okay if I hired him full time. Upon giving him the good news, he said, "My friend is also looking for a job and I only want to come if you'll also hire him." I told him that I had no idea how I was going to pay his salary, no less two salaries. I remember walking by a bookstore that afternoon as I was considering the situation, and seeing a quote in the window: "Leap and the net will appear." So, I leapt, and the net appeared: within a week of hiring both of them, we landed a giant project that we couldn't have possibly completed without them.

A Job from Nowhere

Several years ago, working as a freelance software developer, sometimes I'd get nervous when my bank balance approached zero, which happened on several occasions. Sometimes, even when I was feeling really crappy about that, there were moments of clarity where I was able to tell myself, "Don't worry, just wait." And every time, something showed up, completely unexpectedly.

On one such memorable occasion, a good friend's ex-wife, whom I hadn't spoken to in 13 years, called me and handed me a very, large project on a platter – without asking for a proposal or bid or anything. If I had closed my eyes and dreamed about the most random person that might call me and hand me a project, I guarantee I never would have thought of her.

This is what happens when we *allow* guidance to show up, even if we have no idea where it comes from.

Guidance for an Atheist

Recently, during a workshop I led,

as I shared the notion of guidance, one of the attendees objected, claiming he was an atheist. He put aside his objection for the moment, and when we spoke a couple of weeks later, he said, "I didn't agree with what you said about guidance. But as I thought about it over the past few days, I realized that whenever I've needed anything, it has just sort of shown up." To me, that seems like the best description of guidance that I can think of. It doesn't really matter where that comes from – whether it's God with a big G, or that we're all part of a computer simulation, or just plain coincidence. But knowing *that* the system seems to consistently work in our favor – not *how* it works – is all we really need to know.

Finding Cash in Drawers

In the eight weeks following the heroic gesture of my team offering to work without pay until we could get back on our feet, there were a few occasions on which one of them would come to me, somewhat tentatively, and say, "Umm...Naf, I need to pay my rent." I'd ask what they needed, and they'd say something like "$1200. If you can." I never had an immediate answer or solution. Our bank account was drier than the Sahara. "Give me a few hours," I'd say.

The first time this happened, I remember literally going around the office, looking in drawers for cash, as if there would ever have been any there. But it seemed like doing something was better than doing nothing.

I remember looking through those drawers, knowing there was no *cash* there, but that there *might be an answer* there. I came across a proposal for $9600 that'd we'd submitted to a prospective client several months prior that they had passed on.

I called that prospect and said, "Remember that project we proposed to do for $9600? We can do it for $1200 if you can pay up front." They may have suspected that I had a drug problem, but without much deliberation, they agreed to the stellar deal, and sent me a check immediately, which I was able to give to my employee to pay his rent.

Instead of burdening my team with additional work, I stayed up late nights to complete the project myself.

And then it became a formula. Each time that one of the guys needed to pay their rent, I'd think of someone that I hadn't talked to in months or more, and pull the same "scheme."

What seemed like an unsolvable problem turned into a clever solution that didn't even require much additional work.

Chapter Three

Business Implications

In this section, we'll look at several aspects of business leadership, management, and day-to-day operations, and the potential implications that this understanding provides in those situations.

These discussions are not designed to instruct you as to how to do anything, nor do they aim to encapsulate all of the challenges that businesses face each day. Hopefully, you'll see through these examples that the answer to just about every problem comes from the same place: inside.

The Source of All (Business) Problems and Solutions

A colleague who had recently completed an Executive Coaching program tried to convince me, as many do, that there are "structural problems" within organizations – problems inherent within certain people, processes, systems, etc. – and that to "fix" a company's woes, it's necessary to find, dissect, and re-engineer each of those structural problems.

When trying to solve problems with this "outside-in" approach, we end up playing a game of Whack-A-Mole, whacking down each problem, only to have another (or two or three) arise.

However, when we see that problems don't really exist – they are only an *effect*, or the product of our thinking in the moment – it starts to look a lot less like we need to fetch the toolbox. When we see that problems are illusory and simply made of thought, we automatically gain clarity, and what once seemed like a problem no longer does.

Problems can't be structural. Like the plant in *Little Shop of Horrors*, problems have no life of their own, and only come to life the more we feed them by believing that they are made up of something other than thought. As soon as we stop seeing problems as structural – as things that live on their own, outside of our thinking – they melt away.

Imagine as a CEO, you witness your sales manager and one of your salespeople arguing. One is berating the other about not hitting his quota while the other is lamenting the fact that that's an impossible feat because his sales region has just been hit by a hurricane. As tensions rise, their voices continually get louder until they can't even decipher the words the other is saying.

The more it looks too you, as the CEO, that this situation is problematic, the more it will seem like there is something you need to do to fix it. The more that you see *that it only exists as a problem through your thinking*, the less it will seem like you have to do something to "fix" it. Similarly, to the degree that the salesperson and sales manager see where the problem is really coming from, they will naturally see the humanness of the other. From there, invariably, innovative ideas as to how to meet the quota despite the hurricane will arise, or a new way to measure performance will come into view, or any one of a number of other possibilities will materialize, many of which could have a far more beneficial effect on the company than meeting the quota ever could have.

Please understand that I am absolutely not suggesting any sort of technique. I'm not suggesting that in a heated discussion we should "take a breath," "calm down," or "be empathetic." I'm suggesting that those *effects* will seem to happen effortlessly, to the degree that we see where problems really exist – only through thought!

Most books and articles on corporate culture seemingly point to the same flawed suggestion: create circumstances that will necessarily make people behave a certain way. Some suggest paying an above-market salary and offering platinum level benefits. Others suggest implementing a culture of "no excuses," "3 strikes and you're out," or on the other end of the spectrum, one of "mindfulness" or "kindness." Some promote the idea that a particular office style (open vs. cubes vs. virtual) is what will make your company sink or swim. Pool tables, free lunch, company outings, collaborative performance reviews, "meritocracy," data-driven decision making, a flat management structure, flexible work schedules, beer on Fridays, and on and on the lists go, in a well-meaning but completely misguided attempt to guide us towards a "utopian" culture.

While well meaning, all of these suggestions, whether or not they seem kind or draconian, are pointing in the wrong direction. Those things (policies, for example) are all *effects* of our thinking – they're all "outside." Despite the fact that it often *really, really looks like* these things form our experience, none of them ever can. Because our experience is always created from the inside-out, precisely what prevents amazing cultures from evolving is continuing to fall for the illusion, for example, that we feel great because we have good benefits.

We can no more follow a prescription to create an amazing culture than we can repeat a magic phrase to make someone fall in love with us. We build awesome companies in the same way that we fall in love and build awesome relationships: from the inside-out!

When we point people toward this understanding, what almost always shows up is kindness, creativity, and ultimately all of those byproducts we think we want – like innovation and productivity.

That seems counterintuitive or just plain wrong to most people. Most people would say, of course winning the contract would make you joyous – but that's not true. Some might experience joy for a week, while others might have a joyous moment followed by a period of apathy, while still others may feel panicked thinking about all of the new work that the contract will bring. But, because many of us are under the false impression that, for example, winning a contract could possibly make us happy, we often try to duplicate situations that we believe made us happy at another time. We "go for the win" or have a rah-rah team meeting, "knowing" that that'll make everyone feel great, which in turn will make them do better work. But, of course, that's not how it works.

Some companies, after experiencing some "growing pains" (even though pain can't possibly come from growth, only from our thinking) will institute policies hoping that those policies will alleviate pain or create a feeling that resembles when the company was young, for example, "open communication," "open books," or "beer on Fridays." But when the company was young, the "family" feeling didn't come from a lack of policies (it came from thinking), and that feeling certainly isn't going to return as a result of new policies, either.

Rapport

This book is full of stories and descriptions of the power of rapport. But what is rapport, really?

When we were kids, we were able to make friends quickly and easily. We didn't perceive things like race, gender, preferences, and other things that seem like they can separate us. It was easy to jump into the sandbox and just start playing with someone else, even if we'd never been in a sandbox before. Kids have preferences just like the rest of us, but it's rare that a kid would say something like, "I'm more of a quiet activity kind of person." They do what they're doing, and then move onto something else, without much thought about it.

Just as we've already described so many times in this book, rapport is also an effect of our thinking in the moment. We all have biases and preferences, but unlike kids, as adults, our biases seem very real to us. Often it seems like it's hard to have rapport with someone because of their behaviors, opinions, and preferences. But when we see that our biases are an illusion; that they're *only* created through thought in the moment; and that our thoughts can't possibly define who someone else really is, our biases seem to melt away. We can see that even if it really *seems* like someone is annoying or obstreperous or controlling, it only *seems* that way as a result of *our* thinking in the moment. As we see our biases and preferences for what they really are, human connection happens more easily, and from there, miracles can happen. That is the true definition of rapport.

It's Important. No, Really!

At one company that I worked at, where I managed a team of about 10 software engineers, almost everyone considered every situation that arose to be an absolute emergency. If someone noticed a bug in the software, they'd email me and then run to my desk 5 minutes later to see if I'd read the email. They'd "remind me" how "important" it was and demand to know when it'd be fixed. Or, a high-profile customer would call with a complaint and the "important" alarm would ring.

The effect of "important" had completely worn off.

I shielded my team from all of the "important" noise. When one of these "important" requests came in (at least 6 times a day), I'd assure the requester that their request was on the list and that we'd get to it just as quickly as possible.

As a result, my team and I had great rapport. They knew that I ran interference between them and the constant fires that everyone else perceived. They all had projects that they were working on and by not interrupting them, they were able to continue, and ultimately deliver the products we committed to delivering, on time. And they appreciated the structure they were able to apply to their days.

Once in a while, something happened that actually was important! For example, the application was totally offline or customers were seeing very wrong data. Because we had such great rapport and I'd shielded them from literally hundreds of these "important" interruptions, when I did say that something was important, without having to ask twice, they would literally drop everything and jump to do whatever was needed.

Stop, Drop and Help

During the Great Recession (around 2008), the company I was working at had a major layoff, including one guy from my team. As you probably remember, this recession affected nearly everyone and nearly every company. Companies in our industry and in our area were laying off people left and right.

When I was told that our teammate Sanjay was being laid off and had been asked to leave by the end of the day, I personally rang the "important" bell, quite loudly. I told my team to drop everything; that their only concern for the next several hours was to help Sanjay. In addition to it being a crappy climate in which to get a job, he'd only been working in America for about a year (he was from India) and was on the shy side. He needed our help.

In just a couple of hours, even though it seemed like there were no jobs to be had, every single member of the team was able to provide him with at least one solid job lead or connection to a company or recruiter that was known to be hiring. I was able to help him with his résumé and provide a bit of coaching. Within just a couple of weeks, he'd found a new position.

An Army of Friends

I was on a tour in Jerusalem, on Ammunition Hill, the national memorial to the Six-Day War, with a guide who had been a high-ranking officer in the Israel Defense Forces (Army). He described that the success of the Israeli Army, widely regarded as one of the best armies in the world, comes from the extreme sense of camaraderie among the soldiers.

> He said, "When you see one of your fellow soldiers in a burning building, you don't run in to save him because you have to or because it's your job, you do it out of friendship alone. You do it because he's your friend."

Management

The apocryphal role of the CEO or manager is to set (often arbitrary) goals and then find a way to convince their team to meet them. But what if that wasn't their job at all; rather, the job was to continually point your team towards looking inside themselves and toward their own greatness, and then being wowed by what blossomed?

On one hand, it can seem that typical expectations of a board, CEO or manager are outrageous, in that they expect unrealistic deadlines to be met. Yet, on the flip side, expectations are often set *far below our capacity*. It's impossible for a manager to *know* the collective power of insight of her team. We really have *no idea* of what people are truly capable of. If we, as managers, fall for the illusion that we *do know*, we often sell our employees short. We set "stretch goals" not realizing that we've completely undershot their true capacity. I'm not talking about a capacity for "work." If we ask our employees to dig ditches with nothing but a shovel or call everyone in the phonebook and recite a script, admittedly, we are somewhat limited by time. But I'm pointing to the capacity for an individual, with clarity, to come up with a new idea or completely new way of doing something. For example, a sales person discovering a completely untapped market, or developing his own "sales style" which doesn't precisely follow the company's sales script, but renders far greater results. It's those sorts of discoveries that are *transformational* – *they change everything.*

Managers often wonder, after setting expectations, whether positive incentives (a "carrot" as in a bonus or promotion) or negative incentives (a "stick" as in a demotion or firing) are what drive employee behavior.

But, if you're considering which is the better option, you've fallen for a misunderstanding of what creates human experience (and what drives behavior). Because our experience never comes from something that's happening outside of us, neither the promise of a bonus nor the threat of a firing can make someone feel more compelled to perform. It's impossible. Only their thinking can do that. Inspiration (to perform, for example) is an inside job!

If we can see that even pondering the question of carrot versus stick only creates a cluttered mind, and if we can trust that in any situation we will be guided towards our own wisdom (as will our employees), then we can relieve ourselves from having to come up with a rule for every situation.

Compassion for Meanies

Recently, I was with a friend at a playground, watching her 5-year-old son play. After a while, he came running to her, in tears, complaining that one of the other boys was "hogging" the slide. Her son was convinced that the other boy was being "mean" and "unfair" and hoped she'd intervene. Instead, she gave him a hug (after asking if he wanted one) and asked, "You know how you sometimes have anxious thinking? Do you think maybe he's having some anxious thinking?" And with that, her son went back to the slide and warmly asked the other boy to join him on another part of the playground, which they did without further incident.

Dealing with Bad Behavior

What do you do when someone throws a fit, yells at an annoying customer, repeatedly shows up to work late, or shirks their responsibilities?

What looks like bad behavior to us is a) a reflection of our thinking in the moment; and b) just a symptom of someone's desire to remedy their bad feelings. That desire is rooted in the misunderstanding that bad feelings come from something outside of us – like a crappy customer, an angry boss, ridiculous deadlines, or something else. When someone has that misunderstanding, they often feel like they need to do something to make those bad feelings go away.

In the same way that many of us use alcohol, drugs, promiscuity, or brownies as an antidote to those bad feelings, some people act out. It's that simple. They think that by acting out a particular behavior, they'll feel better. It's absolutely an incorrect assumption, but as long as that bad behavior isn't really endangering anyone, to deny someone who's in pain an antidote is just kind of cruel.

When people think their experience is crappy because of a crappy situation, it's important to remind them that a) they're feeling thought in the moment – things look dark simply because of their *current* state of mind; and b) included in the design of the system is an ebb-and-flow which will carry away that crappy thinking. Often the offender doesn't even think that acting out will make them feel better; they think that acting out will force someone to acknowledge them.

All of us are always behaving based on thinking that seems real to us in the moment. When we see that as true, we're able to see the "offender" as human first, just acting on what seems real. If we really see that, we naturally drift towards love and understanding, to a place of trying to see his world. When his thinking shifts, so will his behavior. There's nothing for us to do but have compassion and wait for the system to fix itself. Good behavior stems from a good state of mind, period. Even if we scream and shout and threaten, his behavior will only change when his thinking does. I'm sure that it sometimes looks like following a punishment (or threat of one) that someone's behavior changes. But, I assure you, that's merely a coincidence.

If we think that having more rules will prevent bad behavior, then we, too, have a misunderstanding. More rules are just more thoughts swirling, which will never lead to a clear mind, and therefore not to better behavior – often worse. The same goes for punishment.

So-called "zero-tolerance" rules are antithetical to creating a world that is more tolerant. In any situation, if we can trust in our ability to know that we will always be able to rely on our intuition to know what to do in that moment, and we have an understanding of why people act out in the first place, why would we ever want to clog up the system with more rules and punishments and blanket decisions?

Neither punishment nor rewards ever cause better behavior or performance.

> ### Take This Job and Shove It!
>
> One day, at a software company I owned, as I was walking out the door to head to a meeting, one of our developers threw a complete fit. He'd been working for months on a project that was not going smoothly. The deadlines were silly, requirements kept changing, and the client had a huge temper.
>
> As I was leaving the office, I saw him stand up, punch his desk, and start cursing as if someone had

wound up a demonic doll. "I'm so f***ing tired of this f***ing sh*t. This project sucks. This client sucks. This job sucks. I f***ing quit." He grabbed a giant trash bag and just started throwing the contents of his desk into it – handfuls of CDs at a time, books, picture frames, sticky notes, and just about everything else on his desk – straight into the trash bag. The entire office was staring at him.

I really wanted to go to my meeting, but I walked over to his desk, and said, "Hey! I get it. This project does suck! I totally get why you'd want to quit. And if you really do want to quit, that's totally cool. I'll give you severance and an amazing reference and whatever else you need, I promise. If you want to quit, it's fine, but please, just don't do it this way."

And as quickly as the storm arrived, it blew over. He didn't say anything. He began to take everything out of the trash bag, piece by piece, and put it back on his desk. We never had a discussion about his frustration, his behavior, or his desire to quit. The project was completed successfully. He never had another similar outburst; in fact, after that, stuff seemed to "roll off" more easily and he got less frustrated and in general, more productive. And he was instrumental in the rescue of our company that I described in the beginning of this book.

I saw him as a guy who was in pain, wrapped up in some junky thinking. As such, being kind is what seemed appropriate to me in the moment. Thankfully, it worked.

The Do Nothing Solution

At a client's company, there was a developer who had been grumpy, cantankerous, and pissed off for weeks. Not surprisingly, his performance had also been poor.

Often, in these cases, it looks like we need to allay their concerns, or offer a carrot or stick, all in hopes that doing so will elicit change in their behavior. But really, listening *alone* is all that's really needed. And it's not even that "listening" is magical, but being with someone, seeing *that they're suffering* (and understanding that their suffering is coming *only* through thought), and sharing in the fact that we're all human and we all get wrapped up sometimes – that's where the power is!

My colleague sat him down, asked, "what's up" and let him talk for 45 minutes, without saying a thing. His mood, behavior and performance drastically improved.

Deadlines, Quotas and Stress

Yes, deadlines and quotas exist. Yes, there's a lot of work to get done, and yes, sometimes it really does need to get done by a certain time. *But that has absolutely nothing to do with the level of stress you experience.*

The origin of the word "deadline" comes from the time of the (American) Civil War. In lieu of a structured prison with walls and bars, a line would be drawn around a prison camp, and if you crossed that line, well, you'd be dead. Hence, "dead line."

We've taken that sentiment of paying the ultimate price and applied it to almost everything that we do. To many people, it seems that by not meeting a quota or deadline, their world and their family's world will come to a screeching halt. *Of course that sort of thinking is stressful!*

Our "fight or flight" system is designed to be engaged *only* when we are facing clear and present danger, for example, when a tiger (or car or guy with a gun) is chasing us. When it's engaged, our physiology changes so that we're better prepared to outrun the tiger or grab a club and attempt to kill it, lest we be killed.

It's an incredibly powerful and effective system, but it's only designed to be engaged once every 24-72 hours for about 30 minutes.

That makes sense. When tigers were chasing us on a regular basis, it makes sense that that sort of situation would happen every one to three days and if you couldn't escape within 30 minutes or so, the jig was probably up anyway. It's incredibly unlikely for any of us that missing a deadline will lead to death or anything even close. Yet, many people activate the flight or flight system for 14 to 16 hours per day!

When the fight or flight system is engaged, our peripheral vision (literally and figuratively), problem solving abilities, creativity, and small motor control are significantly reduced, since being able to hold a pencil or see a bird approaching from the side aren't going to do much good in helping us overcome impending doom. But in business, those are all of the skills that you do need – you need to be creative; you need the ability to see nuance in situations; you need to be able to delicately craft an email! So, being in this stressful state that so many of us see as inevitable is actually damaging not only our health, but our ability to perform!

Modern science incontrovertibly points to living in this stressful state as a being correlated with or a contributing cause of almost every disease. Further, to most of us, the feeling of "being stressed" is quite uncomfortable. Yet, it seems to many of us that there's nothing we can do about it, because it seems like stress is something that's happening "out there," not "in here."

Stress is always a reflection of our state of mind in the moment. If it weren't, then an "insane deadline" would affect you the same way it affects everyone else. Further, if stress came from "out there," then a "ridiculous quota" would affect you the same way in January as it does in June. But, as your thought shifts, which it does all the time, so does your feeling. In January, it may look like a quota is motivating, yet look to your colleague like it's crushing; and in June, it might look the opposite to each of you. And the only thing that creates those feelings is your thinking in the moment.

Let's say your boss tells you a week before the end of the month that your quota for the month has been arbitrarily doubled. To remedy this "horrible" situation, nearly every other bit of leadership advice suggests that you can turn a challenge into an opportunity ("turn lemons into lemonade"). The problem is that that idea seems to imply, "*Of course* doubling your quota is very stressful and a horrible thing to do! But *you* can take *heartache* and turn it into *joy!*" But that's not how it is. It's not a horrible situation that you can choose to see the sliver lining within. It's not a horrible situation until your thinking makes it so! A doubled quota looking like a problem (or blessing) is *only a reflection of your thinking in the moment.*

So, what should you do about these seemingly "stressful situations?" There's really nothing to do except notice that *you are thinking*, and therefore, *you are feeling.* When we notice that the only thing creating our experience in each moment is our thinking, the mind tends to reset itself back to a neutral state.

The Illusion of the Screaming Boss

An edict came from the President of a company I worked at: all "Directors" must carry a Blackberry and respond to email all the time "in case of emergencies." Even without Blackberries, if an email *about anything* had been sent at 11:30PM and hadn't been responded to by the time we got into work, people asked what the hell was going on!

I told my boss that I thought the new rule was unnecessary; that if there were an emergency, he could feel free to call me on my cell phone.

Well, that didn't go over very well.

He stood up, walked around his desk and his linebacker-like frame stood right next to my chair, looming over me. With a bright red face that seemed like it might pop, he screamed at me, "I'm not going to take any sh*t from you, Naf!"

At some point during his rant, something shifted and it really looked to me that this whole thing was made up. The whole idea of emergencies, of control, of immediate response, of bosses and underlings – all made up of thought. I momentarily saw that we are living in an illusory world and that I was bulletproof as long as I understood that "bullets" only exist as a reflection of my thinking. And in that moment, I just started to laugh out loud.

He was a bit shocked, but it seemed like something kind of shifted in him, too, as he looked at me and said, "Yeah, maybe you're right. I'll talk to James [the CEO]."

I promise, I didn't laugh as a way to insult him, or even as a way to make light of the situation. In that moment, it just really seemed like I was watching a silly movie, so I laughed. And maybe in that way, he saw the same "movie" I was seeing.

A Really, Really Big "Oops"

Once, while working on a project for a client, with one click of a button, I accidentally deleted about 20% of the images that had been uploaded by users over the course of several years – tens of thousands of images, including many that were owned by clients that we had licensed the software to. This was, in technical terms, not good.

I emailed the CEO and let him know what I'd done. I told him that I didn't know how to remedy the situation immediately, but if he could give me a couple hours, I'd come up with something. I was calm.

He was upset that I wasn't "taking it seriously," as indicated by the fact that I wasn't running around like my hair was on fire. I asked him, "Would it help?"

He started making contingency plans and figuring out what we'd tell our clients if we weren't able to get the images back.

He wasn't excited about my "no thought" plan, but sure enough, after a couple hours of calm, I came up with a solution, and within a few hours, everything was back to normal, and all of the worry had been for naught.

Productivity

Quite simply, productivity can be defined as the result achieved divided by the effort or time it took to achieve that result. "High performance" can be defined as achieving a lot without a ton of effort.

The problem is, almost every productivity tool out there is good at measuring the volume of work produced, not the result, and therefore, it often looks like more effort, not greater results is what should be rewarded. This happened innocently enough, from the misunderstanding that there's a 1-to-1 relationship between the amount of effort put in and the size of the result achieved. We're left with measurements like "Key Productivity Indicators" that are great at measuring work volume, but don't really help us to produce better results.

Let's consider an example that I'm familiar with: authoring software. A productive team of software engineers would be one that could build a complete product as quickly as possible. What seems to happen repeatedly in software organizations is that programmers scurry like rats and code until their fingers bleed trying to complete an arbitrary set of features in a fixed period of time.

Often, we're so deep chasing several small arbitrary goals that we lose sight of the bigger result we should be chasing. By zooming out, instead of spending hours and hours coding thousands of lines of untested code, we might find a widely used, well-tested module that can be integrated using only a few lines of code. Or, we could find some Open Source software that achieves 80% of the desired result of the entire project! That sort of "productivity hack" isn't a hack at all; it's the kind of ingenuity that comes easily with clarity.

In a customer service organization, we could measure the number of customers serviced in a set period of time, an obvious way to minimize the cost of performing customer service and maximize profit. But, the actual result we desire is to make our customers so happy that they never leave and refer tons of their friends! Does spending the minimum amount of time possible with each customer seem like the way to achieve that?

At Zappos, customer service reps will stay on the phone for as long as it takes to make a customer *happy*. But that doesn't mean it needs to take a long time! Being able to listen (really listen) to a customer's needs and concerns and having the freedom (within reason) to do whatever it takes to make them happy — that's what will achieve the result we're looking for! It's pretty hard to measure all of the tiny interactions with customers that turn them into raving fans. And it's pretty hard to measure long-term benefits (like raving fans and "total customer value") in the short term!

Recruiting and Hiring

All too often a recruiter will try to harness the fire of the company – that very fire that drove you to start the company in the first place – and attempt to translate it into words that will fit well in a job description or on a billboard. More often than not, that fire is reduced to smoke, by describing the same "features" that every other company describes, instead of trying to connect with potential employees on a personal, human level.

When we go on a date, we want the other person to make us laugh, not regale us with their résumé. And we hope to *feel* amazing with them, not analyze their list of attributes to make a sensible decision. So why not approach recruiting in the same way? Connect deeply; fall in love. Don't talk about features.

The more that we think that we have to control the process of connection, the more that we *try to do something* to connect more deeply. To many, that looks like "trying" to be "ourselves," "authentic," "vulnerable," or "interested" – but that's precisely what we don't want to do. Just be: you can't be more or less of yourself no matter how hard you try. The degree to which they perceive our authenticity has *nothing* to do with us and everything to do with *their thinking in the moment*. The exact same conversation with another person, or the same person at another time, would be experienced at least slightly differently.

If we could perceive another human's "actual" authenticity (as opposed to perceiving a reflection of our thinking), the game of the con man would be over immediately. But sometimes our thinking makes it look like a con man is very authentic!

Remember, when you are recruiting, you are *inviting* people to hang out with you, to play in the same sandbox as you, to make giant leaps and experience giant falls with you. You're not collecting resources to do some work for you. Why do many companies use the phrase "phone screen" to describe the initial phase of recruiting? Why come from fear and worry rather than love by using language that reflects keeping people out rather than inviting them in? What might happen if we acted as if she was already our friend or employee? What if we approached every interaction with another human with a clear mind, without expectations, willing to have an open conversation as old friends who've just met?

What if we approached an initial conversation as just that, a conversation: a two-way street where we both just get to learn a bit about each other, as humans? If we did, we could probably "screen" even more effectively than by asking made up questions. But it's hard to have a candid conversation if you're coming from a place of power or desperation. If we speak openly and discover that the fit isn't there, it will become obvious naturally.

To hire "the best", we need to be able to see the best in people. When we aim to uncover the humanity in others, rather than our preconceived notions of what "facts" make the best candidate, we're much more likely to find the "best." When it's not a good match, that will show up clearly too.

Sometimes we get hung up in the thought that a candidate's past equals her future. When we get caught up in our thinking, it's hard to experience the present and see her for who she really is, which really has nothing to do with her past.

You might think that there are certain questions you can ask to determine specific qualities of your candidate; for example, "level of grit," "passion," "integrity," and so on. The challenge is that the entire notion of grit (or laziness, eagerness, passion, etc.) is purely an illusion made up of thought! Further, what looks like "grit" or "tenacity" (desirable qualities) today may very well look like obstinance or an unwillingness to compromise (undesirable qualities) tomorrow, *depending on your state of mind in the moment.* If finding "the best" were as simple as finding those that could most correctly answer our questions, it'd be a pretty trivial task!

We need to understand that during an interview (and always), the way that we see the world is not "real." It's not based on some set of "absolute facts." It's based on *our* set of facts (*our* thinking) which seems real in the moment. What seems like a problem to you may not seem so to your candidate, and what seems like a solution to them may not seem like the right solution to you. **The deeper we understand the notion of separate realities, the more we can focus on seeing their humanity rather than how closely their preferences resemble our own.**

What if we showed up to an interview full of love and genuine curiosity about the candidate, with a deep knowledge that they're a loving creature just like us, and their thinking seems as real to them as ours does to us? What if we knew that there was nothing in particular that we had to ask, and that perhaps by asking a specific set of questions, we could miss seeing a lot? What if we asked every question out of genuine curiosity, not to expose a perceived or potential weakness? Questions like, "What do you know about us?" asked with the intention of sharing and educating, not with the intention of checking if they've "done their homework," can open so many levels of connection.

You might approach recruiting with very worrisome thinking – about the fact that you might hire the wrong person or about what will happen if you aren't able to hire a particular candidate. It is that worrisome thinking that prevents us from connecting, from seeing each other, and ultimately from mutual attraction. The fastest way to "win" employees is to simply share what you believe, from the heart, without expectations of the outcome. It's far easier than coming up with a complicated pitch or throwing cash at them.

Because our reality is created by thought in the moment, people often look different as we get to know them. As we listen deeply, with the same compassion and leniency we'd expect – not listening for the answer we expect to hear, but for what's really inside – we're able to potentially uncover something in them that we, nor they, ever knew was available.

When we see that our experience (during the interview, for example) isn't coming from what they are saying, but from our own thinking, the desire to put their answer into a category or judge it becomes moot. As we continue on a journey with them, we can notice that what we see as "right" or "wrong" can shift with our thinking, sometimes even in the span of a few minutes.

Being "genuine" or "vulnerable" aren't traits to aspire to. When we realize that there's really nothing at stake, our "genuineness," and desire to protect our "vulnerability" naturally melt away.

> ### My Way or the Highway
>
> A friend introduced an engineer with amazing credentials and references to a company I worked with. After an initial contact, he (the engineer) didn't follow up, due to personal reasons that we later became privy to. But at the time, when he was discussed during a meeting, someone said, "He didn't call back, which means that he's not interested, and we only want people who are excited to work here." You see, they painted a picture based on

thought, and believed that picture as if it were true. They knew what they "saw," but misunderstood that our eyes (and other sensory organs) operate more like projectors than they do cameras – they projected the story that seemed real to them.

In this case, it's not necessary to make a rule per se (e.g. to always give someone a second chance). But, if we have an understanding of how the mind works, we always have the potential to see something new in the moment and decide what's appropriate in real time.

Interviewing

Many interviews include at least one session in which we ask the candidate detailed, often technical, questions to ascertain their level of competence. Some interviews seem to be filled with trick questions, sometimes not even directly applicable to the job, aimed at making the interviewer seem smart. In others, there's an open dialog with the candidate, with both the interviewer and candidate continually returning to the (unasked) question of "What can you contribute to help us be better?" It seems with the latter approach, something is often uncovered that we never even conceived of being possible.

I've known many people that really were not good at digging into their brain to find the right answer to some obscure question but could come up with really creative solutions. What if we started an interview by describing an *actual* problem that we're currently having trouble with and ask how she might go about solving it? If we legitimately don't know the answer, she cannot possibly answer correctly or incorrectly. As she develops potential solutions, we can ask her to dig deeper or challenge her on something she's said. We can have a conversation in the exact way that we would if she were already on the job. In this way, we can also expose our own humanity, showing that we, too, don't have all the answers. It's a conversation, through and through – not an interrogation.

Interviewing, like everything else, is mostly about listening. But in order to really listen, you have to consider listening as an active, not passive skill. It's nearly impossible to listen deeply if you're thinking of what to ask next or trying to "evaluate" answers in real time, or typing all of their answers into a "Talent Acquisition Management" software system.

The underpinning of all interviews is the existence of a constant human connection, regardless of each of our preferences. We're all in this together, all the time, even when it looks like we're not.

I'm not saying that a deep understanding of someone's technical skills isn't necessary. I'm saying that through a deeper connection, it's easier to get there without having to ask specific "hard" questions.

If you're in a low state of mind when interviewing, you're much more likely to see what look like faults rather than their magic. Both the candidate and the interviewer are never experiencing what the other is saying or doing; rather, each is experiencing his own thinking in the moment. Approaching the interview knowing that there is literally nothing on the line, and that your job is *only* to bring out the best in everyone, rather than being adept at filtering to find the person who most closely matches your preferences will absolutely revolutionize the way that you discover "the best".

> ### Love Isn't About Attributes
>
> Before I met my wife, I went on a lot of dates (often with the help of an online dating app). I often thought of the parallels between hiring and dating. It's strange how many companies do things in their attempt to attract "talent" that they'd never consider doing if they were dating. When we're looking for a committed romantic relationship, we're really looking for someone to join our "family," much more than for someone to fill our list of requirements. And when we fall in love, it often happens in an instant, and often for reasons that we don't even recognize. We often look backwards and justify falling in love based on something that seems rational. But I know that anyone

who's really honest with herself would admit that there's just a moment that "you know" and that that feeling often comes out of left field.

Sometimes, I'd come away from a date feeling that it had gone really well, and I could easily list a set of attributes of the woman I'd just shared an evening with, e.g., smart, pretty, energetic, etc. Sometimes, when it hadn't gone well at all, similarly, I could list the attributes that bothered me. But when I met my wife, the love of my life, I noticed that after our initial dates, when someone asked about her, I'd have no words, no list of attributes. I'd say, "I can't put it into words... there's just something."

Innovation

Innovation is not a thing we do nor a process we follow. Innovation is an integral part of nearly every aspect of business. In a culture where people really understand how the mind works, ideas that others might call innovative or disruptive will continually be born without having to "generate" them.

Innovation isn't just about creating new ideas for products or services. In nearly every aspect of business, we're continually called upon to be innovative. Solving a difficult issue for a customer on a moment's notice or dealing with complex legal or regulatory challenges requires us to be innovative. Leaping over a technical hurdle that's been plaguing us for weeks also calls for innovation.

There is no process you can follow to be more innovative. Great ideas – product ideas, process improvement ideas, customer service solutions or sales techniques – can happen in an instant, often when we're not looking for them.

Many books about "business innovation" are focused on reverse engineering the tactics and strategies of companies who seem to innovate successfully and are subtitled something like, "How the Big Guys Continually Innovate and Deliver Life-Changing Products." Sometimes companies try to copy (for example) Google's process and wonder why it doesn't work for them. Of course it doesn't work – copying formulas (from the "outside") never works. *Innovation and creativity are an inside job!*

Who knows why Google's innovation "method" works for them. In their earlier days, when they provided employees 20% of their time to explore new ideas, and didn't impose much structure, rules, or expectations around that time, the higher-ups at Google probably had an innate understanding of the fact that "magic" comes from time to explore without much on your mind. Magic comes from inspiration (which can only come from the inside), not process (which is inherently outside). Because innovation only happens from the inside-out, it's actually impossible to reverse engineer!

Have you ever noticed that children rarely need any help exploring or "being creative?" If you drop a pile of Legos in front of a child of almost any age, they'll usually do something clever with them. No kid ever needed to be shown how to draw or color. (Though sometimes we think that we need to show them how to color "properly", but that has nothing to do with innovation, does it?) That's all innovation is – understanding that humans' natural state is one of creativity and with nothing on our minds, and no fear of messing up, we naturally "become" more creative.

To many companies, it looks like the way to be innovative is through brainstorming sessions. But, I promise, there is nothing magical about a brainstorming session. It might look like being in the "mode" of "ideation" was what helped the birth of new ideas, but really, new ideas just show up when the mind is calm. We've all experienced the "phenomenon" (often in the shower) whereby a solution to a problem you've been thinking hard about for days just magically pops into your head. No brainstorming session needed!

As I see it, brainstorming sessions are often not as productive as hoped because of an implied pressure to rescue the company or leapfrog the competition. That sort of noise leads to mental clutter, the opposite of where brilliance is born. What seems to be borne from those meetings are ideas that are unlikely to deliver powerful results. The notion that good ideas can only come from a concentrated "thinking" time is just plain false, and often the best ideas come when we're not thinking!

Across the span of history, the innovations that have most drastically affected our lives or have most effectively disrupted an industry are ones that were original – that is, that were created "from nothing." For example the automobile, iPod, light bulb, airplane, space shuttle, and so on, were not improvements on an existing idea; they were borne from the inside, through thought.

There is nothing "outside" that needs to happen for a brilliant new thought to show up on the "inside." They are unconnected!

Sometimes, a completely formed product idea just comes to you in a dream (while sleeping or awake), without you having to do anything. That is, *you* didn't create that idea – it came from somewhere beyond you. Great ideas don't come from our conscious mind, nor from an iterative process. Iterative processes are great for refining ideas and helping them to blossom, not for "creating" ideas.

At other times, you might start with just an inkling of an idea, but no conceivable idea of how it could turn into a product or business. Yet, fresh thoughts show up to guide you along the path towards completion. We really don't know where these thoughts are created or where they come from, but knowing *that* they show up *dependably*, without us having to *do* anything – that's the cool part.

There is absolutely no correlation between the number of iterations on a

particular idea and the awesomeness or marketability of an idea.

Where have your best ideas come from? Did they show up during a brainstorming session? Or did they show up along a walk in the park, in line at the café, while watching a baseball game on TV, or while in the shower? There have been many times that I've been having lunch with my colleagues or playing video games with them or even just walking to our cars at the end of the day when a solution to a problem that we've been considering for quite some time seemed to appear out of nowhere.

If we want to foster an innovative environment, we simply need to continue to point people in the direction of where creativity comes from as a way to continue to feed the creative fire. We don't even need to analyze and critique their output. We really have no concept of which ideas are actually great, but if we keep adding wood to the fire, I think we'll be surprised by what comes out.

When we are listening, the goal is to listen as a "rock with ears", without judgment, and without an expectation of what we'll hear. Similarly, we can allow creativity to exist on its own, without excessively critiquing its output. Amazing products often looked pretty crappy halfway through their development and it would have been sad if a well-meaning manager had squashed those products because they didn't match up with his thought of what they should look like.

We're often horrible predictors of what will "work." I've been in several brainstorming sessions in which someone proclaimed that an idea was impossible, even though another company had already figured it out! Even highly skilled investors are often horrible at picking "good ideas." Bessemer Venture Partners in San Francisco, who have been involved with at least 117 IPOs, humbly published their "anti-portfolio," a list of companies that they passed on investing in early on, including Apple, eBay, Facebook, Google, Intel, Tesla and others. What if we stopped convincing ourselves that we know and instead were willing to find out?

Doing the Impossible

When I worked as a software engineer, sometimes it seemed as if a requested feature was impossible. I don't mean "hard" or "time consuming" – I mean literally impossible. Sometimes I'd ponder the problem for hours or days, always coming back to the same conclusion.

Other times, I'd start coding the part that I could do, "knowing" that I'd have to stop once I got to the impossible part. I figured if I could show that I did part of it, they'd be more convinced that the rest was impossible. Time after time, after starting the easy part, it's as if the code necessary to complete the "impossible" part bypassed my brain and came from somewhere "beyond" me, straight into my fingers. The really crazy part is that despite that same scenario happening over and over, I never really learned to trust the fact that if I stopped thinking about it, or if I just jumped in to *doing* it (not thinking about doing it), that something that I couldn't have possibly dreamed of would just show up, from somewhere that I couldn't have imagined.

Clarity is where solutions come from, but when we are trying to grit our teeth and think our way out of a problem, our mind is anything but clear.

Chapter Four

Parting Thoughts

Epilogue

So here we are, one hundred pages and a new understanding later.

It's my sincere hope that in these pages you've *seen* something new, a new appreciation for the *nature of thought*, and an appreciation for the magic of the human mind and the countless implications that are on offer for you, your business, family, community, and beyond.

Many people have asked about my process for writing this book. I don't really know how it came together, but I do know that what it looks like now is absolutely nothing like what I thought it would look like when I started. When I started, I had a stack of articles and snippets (well over 100 pages worth) I'd written on culture over the years, but as I started putting them together, what emerged seem way too prescriptive. But perhaps more importantly, I realized that over the course of time, my *way* of seeing the world had significantly shifted.

What I thought that I saw so clearly when I started this book became more and more clear through the process of writing and sharing my message with clients, prospects, and just about anyone who'd listen. The *process* was so powerful that there's not a single word of that stack of articles and snippets left in the book.

As you move forward along this ride we call life, I hope that you come away from reading this book akin to how you'd come back from vacation to a special place you'd never been before: your heart filled with feelings of excitement, hoping to return soon; your belly full of new and wonderful (if not foreign) tastes; and your mind filled with a huge catalog of detailed stories to share, despite not having taken any notes or photographs. Your experience will be preserved in your memory long after your frequent flyer miles expire.

As "situations" arise, I hope that you can look back on your time with this book, and without referring back to it, remember that there was something different, something new, on offer. And from there, perhaps you'll seek that feeling that you remember you had as you so graciously joined me along this journey, from which magic can emerge.

As I sign off, I'd like to leave you with one of my favorite quotes, which reminds me of many of my travels as well as my experience learning "the understanding" and writing this book. I hope to meet you soon.

There's not a word yet for old friends who've just met. - Gonzo *(of The Muppets)*

Epilogue #2: I Have a Dream

I dream of a world in which we truly treat others as we want to be treated and where we are able to see other's views as legitimate as our own, even when that seems to be an impossibility. I dream that everyone can see the love that exists everywhere, and that we gain our power through the love that we have inside, rather than be beaten down by the hate that seems so prevalent in our culture. I dream of a world in which we judge less and love more.

Deep in my heart, I believe that fulfilling this dream will remarkably improve our ability to preserve the planet and its creatures in the long term and to help bring safety, basic needs, and even economic prosperity to those that haven't yet experienced it.

I dream that companies will exist to fulfill a mission that goes far beyond themselves and that they will build cultures in which compensation, benefits, and perks will serve to encourage employees to grow, prosper and enjoy life to its fullest.

I dream that companies will grow to be more ethical; to see that doing so is not antithetical to growth; and to inspire others to do the same. I dream of a world where we don't compromise our ethics to enhance our profits, and where it's second nature to feed the souls and mouths of our employees and every other human that our businesses engage and those that we may never even know about.

I dream that we all will learn to see everyone – employee, vendor, customer, competitor, enemy or friend – as human, first and foremost – and see that we're all made of the same energy. I dream that unions and regulatory agencies will become less necessary as companies learn the tangible and intangible benefits of self-regulation.

What if we put as much energy into making the world better as we do to lining our shareholders' pockets, without having to compromise the latter? What if we really were the change we wanted to see in the world? What if, instead of trying to convince people that helping those less fortunate creates a better society for all of us, we just understand that there can't be a difference between "us" and "them?" To create dividing lines between us only serves to create more separation, which can never be the solution to unity.

I believe so strongly in harnessing the potential of the human mind, combined with the massive amounts of wealth and technology that the human mind has already created, to create a better, more peaceful world for everyone. I believe that global peace is achievable.

And I believe that one of the fastest ways to achieve this dream is through a powerful force called business. But, I can only hope to achieve it through you, the business leaders. With an understanding of what I'm pointing to, not only can you help your business thrive and grow, you can help create a world in which people love their work and start to create a more peaceful, just world. This book is the first step in that direction.

Next Steps

STEP 1

Check out the bonus website for the book: **humansworkingbook.com**. There, you'll find:

- A link to the Facebook group, to discuss the book and its theme. Ask whatever you like, and I or someone else in the community will respond.
- Selected chapters in audio format, read by me.
- A "Culture Self-Assessment" for your company, as well as other tools and resources.
- Lots of additional content, including frequent blog posts.

STEP 2

Visit **humansworking.co** to learn about executive coaching and corporate consulting. I'd be happy to speak with you to see how I could help. Contact us from the website or email me at **naf@humansworking.co**.

STEP 3

Check out **naphtalivisser.com**, where I blog about personal transformation and peace and also share my personal photography and food related projects.

Sources

A few years ago, I was introduced to The "Three Principles of Mind, Consciousness and Thought," as realized and articulated by Sydney Banks (also referred to as the "Inside Out Understanding" or sometimes "Innate Health" or just 3P). I have had so many insights and my life has really changed since seeing this understanding and continues to change to the degree that the understanding deepens. After speaking with some very experienced 3P practitioners and looking back on my life, I see that I've had an understanding of these principles, to some extent, my entire life. I have generally led my life "from the inside out," following my path as I see fit in the moment more so than following someone else's process. Since I was very young, people have told me that I'm very "connected."

More recently, I've discovered the work of Anita Moorjani (anitamoorjani.com) and Dr. Eben Alexander (ebenalexander.com) who, through descriptions of their near death experiences and unexplained healing, have led me to seeing even more deeply that all living things are deeply connected in ways that we have not yet begun to understand.

From there, I have dug into the work of consciousness researchers such as Dr. Pim

Van Lommel, Alan Wallace, Dr. Rupert Sheldrake, and Dr. Russell Targ.

Through these deeper understandings, I have been able to completely forgive anyone from my past and (without actually doing anything) the "reality" of my past (childhood, failed businesses, untoward business partners, etc.) has completely shifted (and mostly "melted away"). As I look toward the present and future of the world at large, I'm now able to easily forgive (and in fact rarely even see the need to forgive in the first place) and have spontaneous compassion, even for people that seem "horrible" to many.

These paragraphs may seem "out there" and may seem to have nothing to do with business. But, nothing could be further from the truth. If we want to succeed in business, whether or not we have an altruistic bent, understanding thought, consciousness, and our interconnectedness is absolutely essential.

Acknowledgements

There are so many folks who have helped me complete this book and I want to credit them for their invaluable contributions:

My amazing wife Michelle, for her never-ending support, encouragement, and willingness to let me explore the future even when it's very unclear where I'm headed. And, in advance, for being the amazing Mom that I know she'll be to our soon-to-arrive child.

My parents, for their continued emotional (and sometimes financial) support in all of my crazy business endeavors and for always trying their damnedest to do the right thing, even when it didn't look like that to me.

My sister Kate, whom I've adored since the day she was born, for being a cool sister and only telling me I'm nuts when I really needed to hear it.

Amro Arida, Saba Ghole, Tim Driscoll, Dominic Chavez, and Adam Steinberg, for their friendship and extreme amounts of creativity, some of which has thankfully rubbed off on me.

Ezra, Delilah, Simon, and Millie, my "junior" buddies who consistently reaffirm the "meaning of life" to me. I love you all so much.

So many mentors and teachers, a couple of whom I've never even met: David Westerman, Dr. Bill Pettit, Michael Neill, Jesse Elder, Dr. Mark Howard, Mara Gleason, Robin Charbit, Dr. Cheryl Burns, Garret Kramer, Dr. Amy Johnson, Dr. George Pransky and Sydney Banks.

The many people who read early versions of the book, often multiple times, and provided outstanding critiques: Ann Graham, Robin Charbit, Martin Croft, Jay Anton, Dr. Cheryl Burns, Dr. Amy Johnson, Christine Higgins, Amir Karkouti, Josianne Fox, Saba Ghole, Jesse Nahan, Setara Campbell, Brian Samuel, Timothy Driscoll, Tara Mazzeo, Linda Pritcher, Sotirios Kotsopoulos, Thomas O'Connell, Louie Balasny, Marty Sirkin, and Stephan Chenette.

David Westerman, who introduced me to "The 3 Principles," read countless versions of the book, and provided an infinite number of micro-pushes in the right direction so I could see something new for myself.

Dr. Paul Levenson, who encouraged me often and led me to many insights, some of which led to writing this book and starting a coaching practice; and for teaching me about "deep listening" when I was only 12 years old.

The entire Furnace Labs team (from the story at the beginning of this book) who taught me so much about business, life and friendship, and who inspired me to pursue this line of work. Also, Jefferson Macklin who helped to make Furnace Labs what it was.

Richard Dean, one of my earliest bosses, who was an oasis in a desert of a company and showed me the power of being a kind manager.

My coaching clients and all of the teams I've ever worked with, some of whom provided fodder for the book and who help me to improve what I do every day.

My Mom, for painstakingly proofreading and editing the final version as well as helping to develop the title. And for always meaning it when she encouraged me to do anything I want.

Amro Arida, for designing the cover and for making a decent-looking photograph of me.

Made in the USA
Columbia, SC
16 March 2018